Knowledge in a Nutshell® on SUCCESS

compiled by

Charles Reichblum

arpr, inc.

Paperbacks

KNOWLEDGE IN A NUTSHELL®
ON SUCCESS

arpr inc., Paperbacks edition/November 2007

For inquiries or to order additional books,
contact arpr inc., 1420 Centre Avenue,
Suite 2213, Pittsburgh Pa. 15219 or call:
**1-800-NUTSHELL (1-800-688-7435) or visit
www.knowledgeinanutshell.com**.
Quantity discounts available.

ISBN: 0-9660991-4-1

Printed in the United States of America.

PREFACE

How did we go about picking the 365 best things ever said about achieving success in work and at home?

Obviously, it's a purely subjective choice—but we culled through thousands and thousands of sayings about success from ancient to current times.

We feel the ones we picked are eternal truths. We feel they are practical today, whether they were said or written years ago, or recently.

Above all, we feel they can be helpful to anyone, at work or in living our daily lives.

You may find a particular favorite here—one that especially rings a bell for you. We urge you to put it on your desk or mirror or refrigerator or at least in the back of your mind, and think about it often.

We suggest you read them all—re-read them often, and think about each one. They may help you feel better, and do better. At least, that's our hope.

Some of the sayings here are from famous authors and thinkers, some are from less-famous people, and some have been collected from unknown sources—but they all passed our test of advice that can help anyone…to make this collection a book to treasure…a book to keep.

DEDICATION

Knowledge in a Nutshell® on Success is dedicated first to the memory of Barbara Rodi, our administrative assistant for over 40 years. Her enthusiasm, optimism and positive attitude contributed greatly to my ability to pursue my research, compilation and writing of my many books and columns.

Secondly, for the support I continue to receive from my wife, Audrey, and our children and grandchildren, Bob, Diane, Rachel and Justin and Bill, Amalie, Noah and Clarissa. They are the source of much happiness and my realization that success in life comes through how we look at ourselves at work, at home and at play.

Knowledge in a Nutshell
On Success

Table of Contents

ONE

ATTITUDE

Success comes in cans—

not in can'ts.

***

A positive attitude is good

medicine--and it's free. You

don't need a prescription to get

it.

The person who has hope,

has everything.

Helen Keller

***

Nobody is born a loser or

born a winner. You are what you

make of yourself.

Lou Holtz

I was always looking

outside myself for strength and

confidence, but it comes from

within. It is there all the time.

Anna Freud

***

Where is the City of Success?

It's in the State of

Mind.

The key to success is to

believe in yourself—and then

act so that feeling is justified.

Joe Lapchik

***

Your most important sale

in life is to sell yourself

to yourself.

A positive attitude can

enhance the value of almost

every experience.

***

If you dare to believe in

yourself, you will act differently

and more successfully.

Life is about 10% of

what happens and 90% of how

you react to it.

Paul Pasqualoni

***

Nothing great was ever

achieved except by those who

dared believe that something

inside them was superior to

circumstance.

Bruce Barton

You have powers you never

dreamed of. You can do things

you never thought you could.

Darwin Kingley

***

Hold a picture of yourself

achieving –and it will help you

achieve.

Dale Carnegie

**Learn to expect, not to
doubt. In doing so, you bring
everything into the realm of
possibility.**

Norman Vincent Peale

***

**Thinking negative thoughts
poisons your mind and limits
your capacity.**

David Sarnoff

There is one thing over which

each person has control—

and that is

their attitude.

Clement Stone

**

The mind is everything.

What we think, we become.

Buddha

Our attitude tells the

world what we think of

ourselves, and what we have

decided to become.

Earl Nightingale

***

Determine to be something

in this world, and you will be

something.

Joel Hawes

It's amazing how much

happier and successful you

become with positive thoughts.

Try it and see.

***

The greatest discovery of

my generation is that humans

can alter their lives by altering

their attitudes.

William James

Fear less, hope more;

whine less, breathe more;

hate less, love more, and better

things are yours.

Swedish Proverb

***

A person rarely hits the mark

or wins the game who says,

"I know I'll miss" while taking

aim.

Arthur Guiterman

Ability is what you're

capable of doing. Motivation

determines what you do. Attitude

determines how well you do it.

Lou Holtz

***

Positive thinking tends to

create positive results by putting

the immense power of the mind

to work in the right way.

Norman Vincent Peale

Attitudes are contagious.

Make yours worth catching.

***

Attitude is the main thing

in being a winner.

Hank Stram

Have a love affair with

life. That is a key to success.

Artur Rubinstein

***

It's not your position that

counts, but your disposition.

TWO

DOING IT RIGHT

It takes less time to do a

thing right than it does to

explain why you did it wrong.

Henry Wadsworth Longfellow

***

The person who is good at

making excuses is seldom good

for anything else.

Mark Twain

To succeed, act as if it were

impossible to fail.

Dorthea Brande

***

Focus on the

important things, and

you can achieve.

Chuck Noll

The average person puts

only 25 percent of their energy

and ability into their work;

the world respects those who put

out more than 50 percent, and

stands on its head for those few

who approach 100 percent.

Andrew Carnegie

The successful person is

the one who does things that

ought to be done.

***

Always put off until tomorrow

what you shouldn't

do at all.

Morris Mandel

The nice thing about

teamwork is that you always

have others on your side.

Margaret Carty

***

Lack of care often does

as much damage as lack of

ability.

Thomas Edison

Failure is often the line of

least persistence.

***

Do the little things right,

for one day you may look back

and realize they were the big

things.

Robert Brault

Do just a bit more than is
expected of you, and you'll be
amazed at the results.

Lawrence Welk

***

To do a common thing
uncommonly well brings
success.

Henry J. Heinz

***

A difficult job is easier to do
if you do it agreeably.

Don't waste your life

in doubts

and regrets.

Oliver Wendell Holmes

***

Make yourself useful, and

you will find that is a key to

success.

You can have more success

in two months by becoming

interested in other people than

you can in two years trying to get

people interested in you.

Dale Carnegie

***

The person who rows the

boat usually doesn't have time

to rock it.

When I stand before God

at the end of my life, I hope

I can say, "I used all the

talents you gave me."

Erma Bombeck

***

Self-respect; self-knowledge;

self-control—these three lead

one to success.

Alfred Lord Tennyson

30

Treat everybody as if

they're somebody, because

they are.

Sparky Anderson

***

A good listener is not only

popular, but after a while he gets

to know something.

Wilson Mizner

You can be a success if you

will only use all your capabilities

--whether they be many or few.

Benjamin Franklin

***

Service is the rent we pay

for the space we occupy on earth.

Augusta Levy

THREE

OPPORTUNITY

When you fail to prepare,

you prepare to fail.

John Wooden

***

Obstacles don't have to

stop you. If you run into a wall,

don't turn around and give up.

Figure out how to climb it, go

through it, or work around it.

Michael Jordan

A failure is a person who

complains of noise when

opportunity knocks.

***

Learn to listen. Sometimes

opportunity knocks very softly.

There may be more

beautiful times, but this one

is ours, so make the most of it.

Jean-Paul Sartre

***

Opportunity is missed

by many people because it is

dressed in overalls and looks

like work.

Will Rogers

Choose a job you love,

and you will never have to work

a day in your life.

Confucius

***

I always try to reach as

far as I possibly can; and if I fall

a little short, then I'm still

farther ahead than if I hadn't

reached at all.

Don Shula

Do the best you can, where

you are, with what you have

today.

Henry J. Heinz

***

It takes as much energy

to wish as it does to plan.

When one door closes,

another door opens; but we

often look so long and so

regretfully upon the closed door

that we do not see the ones which

are open for us.

Alexander Graham Bell

***

Sometimes those who

complain about the way the

ball bounces are the ones who

dropped it.

Alan Reed

There is no

security; there is

only opportunity.

Gen. Douglas MacArthur

***

Build up your weaknesses

--and they become your strong

points.

Knute Rockne

A window of opportunity

usually will not open itself.

Michael Crichton

***

Be prepared. It wasn't

raining when Noah built the

ark.

FOUR

EFFORT

Triumph is just "umph"

added to "try."

***

The right angle to

approach a problem is the

Try-angle.

Bryan Hoddle

You may be disappointed

if you fail, but you can't win if

you do not try.

Beverly Sills

***

Some people are like

blisters. They don't show up

until the work is done.

Doctors recommend that

people do at least a little work

after retirement; employers hope

they'll do a little before.

Robert Fuoss

***

It's better to wear out

than to rust out.

Richard Chamberland

Go the extra mile. It's

never crowded.

***

Only a thin line

separates the successful person

from the unsuccessful. The

difference is often just a

little extra effort, just a little

more positive thinking.

Success comes from doing

--not from hoping.

***

You can't pass anyone

if you stay in a rut.

The world is looking for

people who can do something,

not for those who can explain

why they didn't do it.

E.W. Wilcox

***

By the street of "By and

By," one arrives at the house of

"Never."

G.K. Chesterton

If you want to leave

footprints in the sands of time,

it will be necessary to wear

your work shoes.

***

I only work half a day.

It doesn't matter which half—

the first 12 hours or the last

12 hours.

Kemmons Wilson

No person should be

called a failure until he stops

trying.

***

Nothing in the world can

take the place of

perseverance. Talent will

not. Genius will not.

Education will not. Persistence

and determination are

omnipotent.

Calvin Coolidge

Pray as if everything

depended on God, and work as if

everything depended on man.

Francis Cardinal Spellman

***

Work at every job as if

you were the boss.

Potential doesn't mean

a thing—performance does.

Joe Paterno

***

Take pride in your

work—whatever it is—

and you'll get along

better in the world.

The world is full of willing
people—some willing to work,
the rest willing to let them.

Robert Frost

***

There's always a place in
the world for the person who
says, "I'll take care of it."

Harvey Mackay

You have to sacrifice to

win. That's my philosophy in

six words.

George Allen

***

It's not enough to have

great qualities. We must do

something with them.

Rochefoucauld

Knowing is not enough;

we must apply. Willing is not

enough; we must do.

G.C. Lichtenberg

***

Ideas don't work unless

you do.

We cannot do everything

at once, but we can do something

at once.

Calvin Coolidge

***

You can't climb the ladder

of success with your hands in

your pockets.

Mark Twain

Perseverance is the work

you do after you get tired of

doing the work you already did.

Newt Gingrich

***

Genius is 1 percent

inspiration and 99 percent

perspiration.

Thomas Edison

It's good to put forth a

lot of effort—no one yet ever

drowned in sweat.

Pete Dimperio

***

The three words, "I will

try" have worked wonders.

Joel Hawes

Try, because if you don't

come to bat you can't get a hit.

Robert Ulrich

***

Everyone has untapped

abilities they haven't

used yet.

One disadvantage of

having nothing to do is you

can't stop and rest.

Franklin P. Jones

***

The will to keep going

is often the difference between

success and failure.

David Sarnoff

Nothing is really work

unless you'd rather be doing

something else.

James Barrie

***

"Success" comes before

"work" only in the dictionary.

FIVE

SELF-IMPROVEMENT

What's the biggest room

in the world? The answer: The

room for improvement.

***

You can't spell success

without "U".

Life is like a trumpet.

If you don't put anything in,

you don't get anything out.

W.C. Handy

***

Reading and learning

are to the mind what exercise

is to the body.

Richard Steele

How can an ordinary

person find time for self-

improvement? A single hour

a day, steadily given to the study

of some subject brings

unexpected accumulations

of knowledge.

William Channing

***

An investment in

knowledge pays dividends.

Benjamin Franklin

***

I never learn anything

by talking, but I learn things

when I ask questions.

Lou Holtz

One of the most dangerous

sports you can participate in is

jumping...to conclusions.

***

As you ramble on through

life, whatever be your goal, keep

your eye upon the doughnut, and

not upon the hole.

You must have the will

to win—not just the wish to

win.

Patty Berg

***

Determination is the

down payment on the purchase

of achievement.

William Ward

The only thing more

painful than learning from

experience is not learning

from experience.

Archibald MacLeish

***

Spend as many hours as

you can productively; you'll

have the rest of eternity to

sleep.

It's okay to retire from

a job, but don't retire from

life.

Mary Martin

***

It's better to be 70 years

young than 40 years old.

Oliver Wendell Holmes

If you cannot do great

things, do small things in a

great way.

James F. Clarke

***

If we did all the good

things we are capable of doing,

we would literally astound

ourselves.

Thomas Edison

SIX

WORRY

Worry, like a rocking
chair, will give you something to
do, but it won't get you
anywhere.

***

Don't confuse worrying
and thinking. It's all right to
think.

William Feather

Worry itself won't solve

problems or cure ailments—but

it can produce both.

***

Worries are like gnats.

Movement and activity disperse

them.

J. Gustav White

Instead of worrying about

what you don't have, make the

most of what you do have.

***

How much pain

worries have cost us

that have never

happened.

Benjamin Franklin

Don't worry about just

trying to be better than others.

Try to be better than yourself.

William Faulkner

***

When you have a problem,

think of solutions instead of the

problem.

SEVEN

MAKING MONEY

The word "dough"

begins with "do."

***

Even the woodpecker

owes his success to the fact

that he uses his head and keeps

pecking away until he finishes

the job.

Coleman Cox

Success is discovering the

things you are best at, and then

using them.

***

People will sit up and take

notice of you, if you will sit up

and take notice, of what makes

people sit up and take notice.

Frank Romer

To be a great salesperson,

do something for someone else

every day.

***

Not everyone is willing to

pay the price of success; some

people have a wishbone instead

of a backbone.

J.C. Penney

Lesson for salespeople:

A gossip is one who talks about
others; a bore is one who talks
about himself; a brilliant
conversationalist is one who
talks to you about yourself.

Lisa Kirk

***

Nature made work a
necessity—but attitude can
make it a pleasure.

Successful lives are not

copyrighted. You can develop

your own life into success.

***

A rich man is nothing but

a poor man with money.

W.C. Fields

If you want to be

successful, begin where you are;

don't wait for something that's

future and far.

Priscilla Leonard

***

Don't let what you can't

do interfere with what you can

do.

John Wooden

There's a way to do it

better...find it.

Thomas Edison

***

Here's good career advice:

Find out what you like doing,

then get someone to pay you for

doing it.

Bill Farrell

The best way to get rich

is to enrich others.

Earl Nightingale

***

Realize that success is

available to anyone. It might

as well be yours.

I can't do everything,

but I can do something.

Helen Keller

***

One way to be successful

is to learn to like the things you

have to do.

Johann Goethe

Success is the process

of bringing out the best in

yourself.

Frank Potts

***

You don't have to be a

genius to get by in this world.

Ted Turner

Many things are lost for

want of asking.

***

I wish the buck stopped

here. I could use a few.

EIGHT

WHEN THINGS ARE TOUGH

The real test in golf and in

life is not keeping out of the

rough, but getting out after

we are in.

John Moore

***

The one common

denominator of successful

people is they don't let

failure discourage them.

Paul Harvey

The world is full of
troubles and problems, but
it is also full of goodness and
opportunities. Concentrate
on the latter.

***

It's not how far you
fall, but how well you bounce
back.

George Halas

The same disappointments
in life that will embitter one
person will inspire another
person to overcome them.

***

Ocean tides that go out
come back again. Wise people
who ponder that are not
troubled in adversity.

Here's a secret. Tell
yourself that thousands of
people, no more intelligent
than you, have mastered
problems like those that now
baffle you.

William Feather

***

Never, never, never,
never, never give up.

Winston Churchill

A problem is a chance

for you to do your best.

Duke Ellington

***

When you're down in the

mouth, remember Jonah. He

came out all right.

Thomas Edison

Don't forget the world is
round, so the place which may
seem like the end, may also be
only the beginning.

Ivy Baker Priest

***

Problems are only
opportunities in work
clothes.

Henry J. Kaiser

The way I see it, if you

want the rainbow, you gotta

put up with the rain.

Dolly Parton

***

By making the best of

things, we make the best of

of ourselves.

90

When everything seems to

be going against you, remember

that the airplane takes off against

the wind, not with it.

***

We are all capable of

greater things.

Horace Walpole

One of the best medicines

a person can have is hope.

O.S. Marden

***

You're on the road to

success when you realize that

failure is merely a detour.

William Milnes Jr.

Past failures should be

regarded only as lessons of

learning, not crippling

disasters.

Dr. Jean Rosenbaum

***

A person is not finished

when he's defeated; he's

finished when he quits.

Little minds are tamed

and subdued by misfortune,

but great minds rise above it.

Washington Irving

***

He who does not hope to

win has already lost.

Jose Joaquin Oimedo

If you can't make your

life easier, then make yourself

stronger.

***

When the going gets

tough, the tough get going.

Knute Rockne

Great people choose to be

greater than their problems.

Mark Hansen

***

Don't part with your

hopes. The person who has

hope still has a chance.

Mark Twain

Anybody can slip and
fall down in life; what you
must do is get back up and keep
going.

Vince Lombardi

***

People become great when
they are able to rise above
defeat.

Ted Turner

In trying times—don't

stop trying.

***

Don't hope without

doubt—and don't doubt

without hope.

Lucius Seneca

You can't let problems

beat you, because you're

going to have them

no matter what. So learn

to overcome them.

***

Always remember the lines from

William Henley's famous poem:

"I am the master of my fate; I am the

captain of my soul."

There is really only one

failure in life, and that is not

to do the best you can.

Charles Buxton

***

Don't ever despair, but if

you do despair, work in despair.

Don't ever quit.

Ralph Waldo Emerson

NINE

FEAR

Nobody can make you

feel inferior without your

consent.

Eleanor Roosevelt

***

He who undervalues

himself is usually

undervalued by others.

William Hazlitt

If you're afraid to lose,

you'll often lose; if you hate to

lose, you'll often win.

***

Never let the fear of

striking out get in your way.

Babe Ruth

***

Stand up to fear.

You're bigger than it is.

Norman Vincent Peale

The greatest fear is the fear

that life has no purpose. You are

here for a reason. Find it;

capitalize on it.

***

Don't ever be afraid to

look somebody in the eye. You

are just as good as anybody.

Sarah Delany

The greatest mistake you

can make is to be continually

fearing that you'll make one.

Elbert Hubbard

***

Don't crucify yourself

between these two thieves:

Regret for yesterday and fear

of tomorrow.

Fulton Oursler

Fear is a darkroom where

negatives are developed.

***

Fear nobody—

but respect everybody.

Tom LaSorda

***

If you can conquer your

fears, you'll add success to your

years.

TEN

GOALS

You gotta have a dream;

If you don't have a dream, how

you gonna have a dream come

true?

Oscar Hammerstein II

***

They can win, who believe

they can.

Virgil

Usually the best way to

make your dreams come true

is to awaken from your dreams

and start working on them.

***

Goals are dreams with

deadlines.

Diana Scharf Hunt

Success is often only an

idea away.

***

The trick in life is to decide

what's your major aim. Once

that is settled, you can get on

with the orderly process of

achieving it.

Stanley Wilson

The important thing is not
who you are or where you've
been, but what you are, and
where you're going.

***

Life isn't all you want, but
it's all you have—so make the
most of it.

The world stands aside to

let anyone pass who knows where

they are going.

David Jordan

***

Be a success-seeker

rather than a

failure-avoider.

Tom Dargan

Don't be afraid to dream

big dreams.

Ben Feldman

***

Happy are those who

dream dreams—and then are

ready to make them come

true.

Leon Suenens

The real tragedy in life is

not being limited to one talent,

but in the failure to use that one

talent well.

E.W. Work

***

If you aim for nothing,

you'll hit it.

Yogi Berra

Changing one thing for the

better does more good than

talking about a dozen things that

are wrong.

Ann Reyher

***

When you're through

changing, you're through.

Bruce Barton

Failure is not necessarily

missing the target, but aiming too

low.

J.G. White

***

As long as you're going

to be thinking anyway, think

big.

Donald Trump

**Set goals in life. You can't
get there if you haven't got a
destination.**

Harvey Mackay

***

**Keep true to the dreams
of your youth.**

Johann Schiller

ELEVEN

RISK

Without risks, you will

suffer no defeats. But you will

also win no victories.

Winston Churchill

***

Some people have a

thousand reasons why they can't

do something when all they need

is one reason why they can.

John Newbern

To be successful,

knock the "T" off the word

"can't."

George Reeves

***

Keep on going and the

chances are you will stumble on

something—perhaps when you

are least expecting it.

Charles Kettering

If no one ever took risks,

Michelangelo would have

painted the Sistine floor.

Neil Simon

***

Yes, risk-taking can be

failure-prone. Otherwise it

would be called sure-thing

taking.

Tim McMahon

Behold the turtle: He makes progress only when he sticks his neck out.

James Conant

***

Use the talent you have; the woods would be almost silent if no birds sang except those that sang best.

Henry Van Dyke

He who postpones making

the most of his life is like the man

who waits for the river to run out

before he crosses.

Horace

***

You miss 100 percent of the

shots you never take.

Wayne Gretzky

TWELVE

LUCK

Don't depend on a rabbit's
foot for luck. Remember, it
didn't work for the rabbit.

R.E. Shaw

***

The surest way to go broke
is to sit around waiting for a
break.

You've got to be in

position for luck to happen.

Luck doesn't go around

looking for you.

Darrell Royal

***

To be lucky, let your

hook always be cast. In the

stream where you least expect

it, there may be fish.

Luck is when preparation

meets opportunity.

Branch Rickey

***

Remember that every day

has new opportunities.

Pablo Casals

Luck is a very good

word if you put a "P" in

front of it.

***

Good luck is often with

the person who doesn't include

it in his plan.

THIRTEEN

THE PAST

Even God cannot change

the past, so why should you try?

Concentrate on the present and

future.

***

My interest is in the future

because I'm going to spend the

rest of my life there.

Charles Kettering

Yesterday is history;

tomorrow is a mystery; today

is a gift. That's why it's called

the present! Use it well.

***

You can't turn back the

clock on your life, but you can

wind it up again.

Bonnie Prudden

The person who wastes

today fretting about yesterday

will waste tomorrow fretting

about today.

Philip Raskin

***

The past is fine. But we

can't live there.

Irving Berlin

Remember that although

the past cannot be changed, the

future can.

Benjamin Franklin

***

A person is wasting

life force every time he talks of

failure, hard luck, troubles,

past mistakes. Let him turn

his back on the past and face

the present.

O.S. Marden

Don't let your yesterdays

use up too much of today.

Will Rogers

***

When all else is lost,

the future still remains.

FOURTEEN

RESPONSIBILITY

Life is like a cafeteria.

There are no waiters to bring you

success. You have to help

yourself.

***

We shouldn't say the world

owes us a living. The world owes

us nothing. It was here first.

Mark Twain

Taking responsibility,

or seeking it out, is the key

to growth and success.

Louise Bushnell

***

Success or failure are

not chosen for us. We choose

them for ourselves.

Hamilton Mabie

The best helping hand I

ever got was at the end of my

own arm.

***

Trying to make one's self

better is an occupation that ought

to last a lifetime.

Queen Christina

To become what we are

capable of becoming—that is

the purpose of life.

Baruch Spinoza

***

If you take pride in your

work, you will find that people

will then respect you more.

Have you ever noticed that

the knocker is always outside the

door.

Red Foley

***

"Now" is one of the best

words in the language if you

want to improve yourself.

Most people operate on

less than half their power.

George Allen

***

Our job in life is not to

get ahead of others, but to get

ahead of ourselves.

Steward Johnson

It is our responsibilities—

and not ourselves—that we

should take seriously.

Peter Ustinov

***

This time, like all other

times, is a very good one if we

but know what to do with it.

Ralph Waldo Emerson

Success in life comes

not necessarily from doing

extraordinary things—but in

doing ordinary things

extraordinarily well.

John Molnar

***

It's not what happens to

you, but the way you take it

that counts.

Hilys Jasper

You are you—and that's

all you need to be.

***

The day you take complete

responsibility for yourself, the

day you stop making excuses,

that's the day you start to

succeed.

Ladder of achievement:

100% I did.

90%   I will.

80%   I can

70%   I think I can.

60%   I might.

50%   I think I might.

40%   What is it?

30%   I wish I could.

20%   I don't know.

10%   I can't.

0%   I won't.

FIFTEEN

ENTHUSIASM

A smile is the shortest

distance between two people.

Victor Borge

***

Enthusiasm is one of the

most beautiful words on earth.

Christian Morganstern

Go all out no matter how bad
things look because if you keep
hustling, something good will
happen.

Joe Paterno

***

Life is never dull
for the person
with enthusiasm.

If you look forward to doing

your job, you're in danger of

becoming successful.

***

To be successful, the first thing

to do is fall in love with

your work.

Sister Mary Lauretta

142

Fortunate adults put the same

energy and devotion into their

work as children do into their

play.

***

Your expression is one the most

important things you wear.

Sid Ascher

Think success. Act successfully.

When? Now!

***

I wake up each morning

convinced that something

exciting will happen.

Elsa Maxwell

If your work is not fired with enthusiasm, your employer might fire you with enthusiasm.

John Mazur

***

The secret of people who are universally interesting is that they are universally interested.

William Dean Howells

Cheerfulness helps people—

both those who give it and

those who receive it.

Dr. Karl Menninger

***

Make each day

your masterpiece.

Life owes us little;

we owe it everything.

John Mason Brown

***

Today is the first day of

the rest of your life.

Make the most of it.

SIXTEEN

BEHAVIOR

The easiest way to break

a bad habit is to drop it.

John Williams

***

If you don't take care of your

body, where else are you

going to live?

A dishonest act is like a

boomerang. It will circle

about and eventually hit you.

Earl Nightingale

***

The best thing you can

give yourself is

self-respect.

Here's a good habit to get into:

practice self-discipline of

some kind every day.

***

The only discipline that lasts

is self-discipline.

Bum Phillips

Two things that cause failure

are a hot head and cold feet.

O.B. Cooper

***

Failures are divided into two

classes—those who thought and

never did, and those who did and

never thought.

A key to success is to

go through life being a good

friend to yourself—and

to others.

***

My philosophy is very simple.

If you don't like people,

you get the worst of it.

Art Rooney

If you wish to travel toward

success, travel light. Take off

your envies, unforgiveness

and fears.

Glenn Clark

***

It's just as easy to form a

good habit as it is

a bad one.

William McKinley

Make the most of yourself,

for that is all there is

of you.

Ralph Waldo Emerson

***

The greatest thing you can do

is to make yourself a better

person than you were.

Forgive and forget;

sour grapes make

a bad beverage.

***

Always forgive your enemies;

nothing annoys them so much.

Oscar Wilde

Too many people overvalue

what they are not, and

undervalue what they are.

Malcolm Forbes

***

Be yourself. If you start copying

somebody, you'll wind up doing

a second-rate job because that's

what a copy is—a second-rate

version of something.

Chuck Noll

Try not first to become a person

of success—but try to become a

person of value, and then success

will be yours.

Albert Einstein

***

Make friends before

you need them.

Life is what we make it;

it always has been, and always

will be.

Grandma Moses

***

The main person in the world

who can make you successful

is you.

Benjamin Franklin

Always do right. This will

gratify some people and

astonish the rest.

Mark Twain

***

A closed mind, like a

closed room, can become

awfully stuffy.

A person can improve

their looks by merely

being more cheerful.

***

A chip on the shoulder

is too heavy a piece

of baggage to carry

through life.

John Samuels

If you really want the last word

in an argument, try saying,

"I guess you're right."

***

When you're right, you can

afford to keep your temper,

and when you're wrong,

you can't afford to lose it.

J.J. Reynolds

Here are some exercises NOT to do: jumping to conclusions; flying off the handle; running down the boss; and dodging responsibility.

***

Keep cool and you command everybody.

St. Justin

Life is a lot like tennis.

Those who don't serve well

end up losing.

***

Carry yourself with dignity,

and others will accord

it to you.

K.C. Jones

What counts is not necessarily

the size of the dog in the fight,

but the size of the fight in

the dog.

Dwight Eisenhower

***

Show me a person who is a

good loser and I'll show you

a person who's playing golf

with his boss.

Trust yourself. You know more

than you think you do.

Dr. Benjamin Spock

***

Everyone has untapped

abilities they haven't used

yet.

There's no more miserable

person than one in whom

nothing is habitual but

indecision.

***

The mind is like a parachute.

It only functions when

it is open.

Be yourself. Who is better

qualified?

Cole Porter

***

Make yourself

worth knowing.

Fiorello La Guardia

One of the least productive

items manufactured is

an excuse.

***

Correction does much, but

encouragement does more.

Johann Goethe

Live your life so you can

always look anybody

straight in the eye.

Billy Richard

***

If you can be good,

why should you be

bad?

Roberto Clemente

SEVENTEEN

PEACE

Believe that life is worth

living, and your belief

will help create the fact.

William James

***

The person who has a "why"

to live can bear almost

any "how."

Frederich Nietzsche

To know even one life has

breathed easier because

you lived—this is to have

succeeded.

Ralph Waldo Emerson

***

A person can make

something of themselves

no matter what their

station in life.

I forgive myself for having

believed for so long that

I was never good enough

to have, get, or be what

I wanted.

Ceanne DeRohan

***

I can't do everything—but

I can do something with

my life.

E.E. Hale

Grant me the serenity

to accept the things I cannot

change; the ability to change

the things which should be

changed; and the wisdom

to know the difference.

***

If you get the best out of

yourself, you can go to bed

at night in peace.

How do you recover from

severe setbacks? You do it by

meeting them and going on,

and from each you acquire

additional strength and

confidence in yourself

to meet the next one

when it comes.

Eleanor Roosevelt

Children wish they were old.

Oldsters wish they were young.

That's wrong. Accept what you

are and make the best of

yourself, whatever your age.

***

The mind can make goodness

out of badness or badness out

of goodness.

John Milton

Like yourself. If you don't

like yourself, how could

anybody else?

***

Remember that life is like

football. Neither has many

undefeated seasons. But win or

lose, both are supposed to be fun.

Al Neuharth

Remember, you are a child of
the universe, no less than anyone
else, and so you, too, have a right
to be on earth and be successful.

Max Ehrmann

***

You're the last person you
should give up on.

If you can choose between
association with optimistic or
pessimistic people, stick with
the optimists. Life will be better.

James Reston

***

The person with the proper
outlook on life has nothing to
fear in life or in death.

Socrates

Don't waste time doubting

and fretting. Spend your time

believing and doing.

Marvin Loren

***

You can't smile and feel

depressed at the same time.

Try it and see.

Dr. Harry Margolis

Nothing helps you to be on

good terms with others

more than to be on good

terms with yourself.

***

You'll find your life will be

better if you're always a

little kinder than is necessary.

James Barrie

Two men look out of the same

window; one sees mud, and the

other sees the stars.

Frederick Langbridge

***

Remember, we are all

good for something. Find

it in yourself and others.

The longer we dwell on our
misfortunes, the greater is
their power to harm us.

Voltaire

***

Those who bring sunshine to the
lives of others cannot keep it
from themselves.

James Barrie

If you are feeling sorry for

yourself, you are building a

wall which shuts you out from

the things you desire.

Edward Hale

***

A smile is contagious—be a

carrier.

When we seek to discover the

best in others, we somehow

bring out the best in

ourselves.

William Arthur Ward

***

`Do not do what you would

undo if caught.

You'll like your life better

if you simply decide

to enjoy it. Try it.

It's true.

***

Pessimism is an enemy.

Optimism is a friend,

because it creates possibilities.

Tommy Lee Jones

Being defeated is often a

temporary condition.

Giving up is what makes

it permanent.

Marilyn vos Savant

***

If you don't get bitter,

you've got a chance

to get better.

Curley Hallman

A dispute has two sides—

but make sure it also

has an end.

***

Every day is a new leaf

in the Book of Life.

With every rising of the sun,

think of your life as just

begun.

***

Any day of the year is a good

day to start improving

one's self. Why not today?

Order Additional Books As Gifts

Knowledge in a Nutshell on Success
(ISBN 0-9660991-4-1)
Quantity _____ @ $9.50 each
Total _____
Add $2.50 for shipping & handling for first book
and 50 cents for each additional book.
                                Grand Total _____

(Discounts available for quantities over 100)
Send check or money order to Knowledge in a
Nutshell Inc., 1420 Centre Avenue, Suite 2213,
Pittsburgh Pa., 15219, or for credit card orders,
call 1-800-NUTSHELL (1-800-688-7435) or
visit www.knowledgeinanutshell.com.

Name _____
Address _____
City/State/Zip _____

For information on ordering any of the
other Knowledge in a Nutshell books,
call 1-800-NUTSHELL (1-800-688-7435)
or visit www.knowledgeinanutshell.com.

**Discounts are available for those wishing the
set of Knowledge in a Nutshell books, or for
quantities of individual books).**

OTHER BOOKS IN THE SERIES

*Knowledge in a Nutshell...*over 500 amazing
fun facts and stories on U.S. Presidents, Movies,
Music, History, Health, Money and much
more...Find out about the one man present when
THREE U.S. Presidents were assassinated...
which U.S. state no longer exists...Why the
Oscars are called Oscars.

Knowledge in a Nutshell on Sports...
Find out about the 6-inch home run...Why golf
courses have 18 holes...The great football team
that never existed.

*Knowledge in a Nutshell on Popular Products
Heinz Edition...*Over 500 amazing food facts
and international recipes...Why ketchup is called
ketchup...All the ways vinegar can help you
around the house...Why hamburgers are called
hamburgers—even though they have no ham in
them.

Knowledge in a Nutshell on America...
The amazing story of the real Uncle Sam and
his boyhood friend...Surprising stories about our
patriotic songs... How each state got its
name...The perfect handbook on America.

Quantity Discounts Available
Call 1-800-NUTSHELL (1-800-688-7435) or
visit www.knowledgeinanutshell.com.

THE EDIBLE GAME A SMART COOKIE™

**The perfect food for a hungry mind...
You can't eat just one--you'll want to know
more and eat more...There are cookies and
there are games—this gives you both.**

America's answer to the fortune cookie,
this walnut-shaped cookie has a fascinating
question-and-answer in each one. The only
game where you can eat the game board.

One too many fortune cookies convinced
Charles Reichblum, author of the *Knowledge in a
Nutshell*® series, that there was a better way to
entertain people after a meal, so he created the
Q&As.

The cookie, designed by international
architect, Sylvester Damianos, FAIA, and baked
by Jenny Lee Bakery, a 75-year-old Pittsburgh,
Pa. bakery, is available in a box of 12
($ 14.95 US + s/h) or 20 individually-wrapped
cookies in a tub (24.95 US + s/h).

TO ORDER: call 1-800-NUTSHELL or via
www.knowledgeinanutshell.com.

Bulk orders and custom questions available for
special occasions.

Printed in the United States
203636BV00002B/13-33/A